DOLPHIN GIRL

by Stephen Bedwell JR

Illustrated by Zuzu

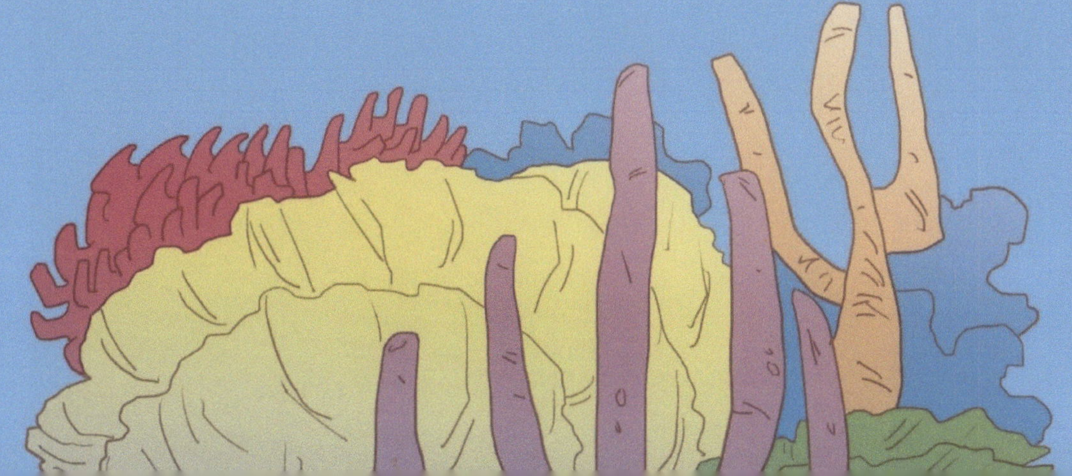

DEDICATION

To Willow:
May we always love, dream, and enjoy a warm, clean ocean.

Rise and shine!
Today, I feel quite fine.
I take a giant yoga stretch.
Then a glass of water I must fetch.

Water is very important to start the day.
I even love to start with some fresh squeezed O.J.
We must keep our bodies hydrated with healthy liquids.
This includes grandmas, aunties, moms, dads, and us, kids.

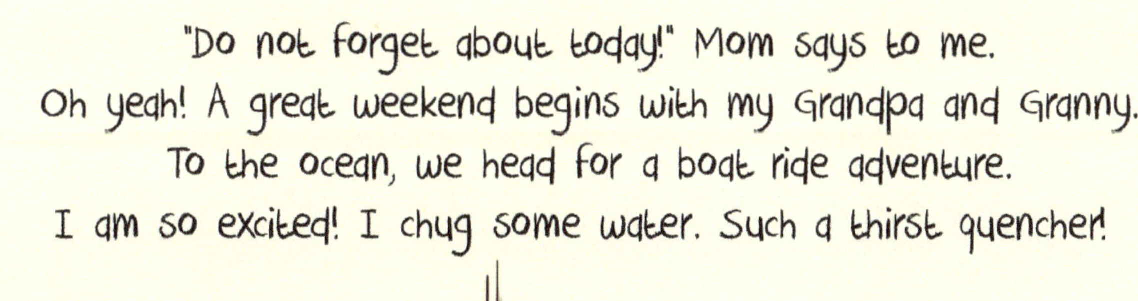

"Do not forget about today!" Mom says to me.
Oh yeah! A great weekend begins with my Grandpa and Granny.
To the ocean, we head for a boat ride adventure.
I am so excited! I chug some water. Such a thirst quencher!

Grandpa and Granny will be meeting us down by the coast.
Mom asks me, "What do you think you will enjoy the most?"
I tell her it will be great to ride on a boat.
And swim like a fish in the ocean and float.
I am really hoping to see a friendly dolphin.
And feel the warm sun upon my youthful skin.

There they are!
It is Grandpa and Granny!
They are in front of
a big boat waving at me!
I hang out of the window
and quickly wave back.
This causes me to spill
some nuts I am having
for a snack.

"Hello! Hello!" Granny welcomes us to the dock.
She says, "We will be setting sail at 12 o'clock!
First, we must fill the boat with some yummy food and sheets for your bed."
Granny takes out a hat and places it on my head.
I will need it for protection from the hot sun.
It is made from hemp and I love it a ton!

I run over to help Grandpa with a box.
"Oh my!" I scream out. "This is heavy! What is inside it, rocks?"
Grandpa tells me it is full of fresh fruits and vegetables.
He tells me that when traveling, it is vital to have them on our tables.

I ask Grandpa what types of foods he has packed.
He explains he has only brought those that give a positive impact.
"We always want our bodies and the Earth to be healthy.
We want the animals to always be loved and live free."

Bananas, melons, grapes, oranges, and greens.
Dates, potatoes, quinoa, rice, and beans.
All these we will eat as we explore an ocean so vast and wide.
What a great trip it will be as we glide and ride the ocean tide!

We are all packed up and ready to set sail.
I wave to Mom as I eat some chips made of kale.
The salty ocean air blows upon me and I take a big inhale.
I feel happy and at peace as I slowly exhale.

Toward the back of the boat, I hear some commotion.
Grandpa is leaning over into the ocean.
He is picking up a plastic bottle and a bag.
It seems to have gotten into our motor and created a snag.

Granny tells me that the ocean holds a lot of pollution.
She continues by saying, "However we are the solution.
Try not to buy plastic and be sure to recycle always.
Be mindful and pick up trash, but do not slack on any days.
Put only plants in your dish.
Never ever eat any fish."

Out on the ocean water,
The sun seems to get a little hotter.
Granny asks me to help with dinner preparation.
I say, "Certainly, but first I need some hydration."
We drink water straight from a coconut.
Then gather some fresh fruits and veggies to cut.

We are going to have some orange slices, grapes, and a salad of beans.
The beans will be mixed with grapes, corn, celery, cucumber, and greens.
It will be a great, healthy whole food, plant-based meal.
Amazing and refreshed is what it will make us feel.

Chopping and tossing, it all looks so yummy!
I can hear the grumbling and rumbling in my tummy.
Granny makes such wonderful and amazing food.
Her good food always puts me in a happy mood.

We take a moment to feel the love within and around.
It is a moment of silence, we are still and don't make a sound.
The waves make the boat bob down and up.
I hope the water doesn't spill out of my cup!

Oh my! I am so full from this delicious meal.
All that is left on the table is an orange peel.
I lean back and take a big stretch.
What is that thing that my eyes catch?

Look, it is a huge boat! Granny says her friends are aboard.
They work hard and leave no part of the ocean unexplored.
They protect every fish and animal; that is their goal.
Day and night, they are always out on watchful patrol.
They clean the water and make sure no harm is done.
It is a lot of hard work, but also fun in the sun.

We take a moment to stop and greet.
Their boat sure is large and neat.
They picked up a lot of trash in the ocean today.
And even stopped someone from harming a shark in the bay.

We wave goodbye as the sun has just about said goodnight.
Pretty soon the moon and stars will be our only light.
Making my way to bed, I will sleep with the smell of ocean air.
Maybe in the morning I will have a nice dream to share.

I awake to some noise and water splashing.
I sure hope the boat is not crashing.

I jump out of bed and race to the deck.
I hope everything is okay; I need to check.
I look upon the water and suddenly freeze.
I become hit with a strong ocean breeze.

I hear a whistle and
look to the right.
A dolphin startles me
as it takes to flight.
It crashes down in the water,
splashing me wet.
I walk to the edge and
see it is caught in a net.

I reach down and grab the net
with all of my might.
The moon and stars are in the sky
to provide me with light.
Shaking and pulling, I hope it gets free.
I hear the dolphin say, "Please help me!"

I am shocked that the dolphin is talking to me.
Pulling harder, I get on one knee.
The net is now just about over its neck.
I pull really hard. It lets loose and I fly to the deck.

The dolphin says, "Thank you for all your hard work!"
I can't believe it is talking. I let out a nervous smirk.
The dolphin explains that the oceans are being
emptied of life from being overfished.
Not getting caught in nets is something the fish
and animals have always wished.

The dolphin asks me to hop on his back and take a ride.
He will take me around the ocean and be my guide.
I hop on his back with a happy smile on my face.
We take off lightning fast as if running a race.

Dolphin shows me fishing net after fishing net.
Seeing fishes caught in them makes me upset.
Dolphin takes me to the water's edge.

And shows me all the farm runoff sludge.
Chemicals used on the land make their way to the ocean.
Dolphin says to "go organic!" It is a better notion.

Next, we visit coral reefs
where there is lots of life.
I learn that here, there has been lots of strife.
Dolphin tells me they are not as large
and beautiful as in the past.
Overfishing and pollution has made it
become such a contrast.

We head back to the boat and I ask, "What can I do?"
Dolphin explains that I can help clean the oceans too.
Do not eat animals and seafood, but eat only plants.
That way, the fish and animals can live happy lives and dance.
Every time I eat I can choose plants and love.
It will make a difference to those in the water and those above.

I awake and think about all I have learned and how it was fun.
I yawn really big and step out into the rays of the morning sun.
Granny bear hugs me good morning and whispers, "It's great to be healthy!"
I hug her back and respond, "And always clean up the ocean, I agree!"

We sit on the deck with melon in our laps.
We watch a dolphin as it jumps and slaps.
It is a wondrous sight to see and enjoy.
"Thanks for the lovely trip, Grandpa and Granny!" I said with joy.

About the Author

Stephen Bedwell Jr. is a Certified Holistic Nutrition Practitioner who educates children to eat a healthy whole food plant-based diet and encourages children to be environmentally friendly. He achieves this through creative and poetic stories that tug at the hearts and minds of children. Stephen lives in Wisconsin, but always finds time to travel to and enjoy the ocean.

Be sure to enjoy Stephen's other great books:

Sunflower Kid
Stan the Plant-eater
Stan the Plant-eater: A Trip to the Garden
Stan the Plant-eater: A Trip to the Fruit Market